How To Invest In Real Estate

The 8 Things You Should Do For Real Estate Investing Success

Adell Paltrow

© 2019 by Adell Paltrow. All rights reserved.

All rights reserved. No part of this book may be reproduced in any form without permission in writing from the author. Reviewers may quote brief passages in reviews.

Disclaimer

No part of this publication may be reproduced or transmitted in any form or by any means, mechanical or electronic, including photocopying or recording, or by any information storage and retrieval system, or transmitted by email without permission in writing from the publisher.

While all attempts have been made to verify the information provided in this publication, neither the author nor the publisher assumes any responsibility for errors, omissions, or contrary interpretations of the subject matter herein.

This book is for entertainment purposes only. The views expressed are those of the author alone, and should not be taken as expert instruction or commands. The reader is responsible for his or her actions.

Adherence to all applicable laws and regulations, including international, federal, state, and local governing professional licensing, business practices, advertising, and all other aspects of doing business in the US, Canada, or any other jurisdiction is the sole responsibility of the purchaser or reader.

ISBN: 9781097167180

Table of Contents

Table of Contents

INTRODUCTION 1

ABOUT THE BOOK 4

WHAT IS REAL ESTATE? 6

IS REAL ESTATE A GOOD INVESTMENT? 16

TYPE OF REAL ESTATE INVESTING 19

    RESIDENTIAL REAL ESTATE 19

    FIX AND FLIP PROPERTIES 20

    COMMERCIAL REAL ESTATE 20

    RETAIL SPACE 21

    INDUSTRIAL REAL ESTATE 22

    LAND 22

    MOBILE HOMES 23

EARNING MORE ON THE SIDE 24

VARIETY OF WAYS TO INVEST IN REAL ESTATE 31

    LONG-TERM RESIDENTIAL RENTALS 32

    LEASE OPTIONS 35

    HOME-RENOVATION FLIPS 39

    CONTRACT FLIPPING 44

    SHORT SALES 45

- Vacation Rentals 47
- Hard-Money Lending 48
- Commercial Real Estate 49

8 STEPS TO REAL ESTATE INVESTING SUCCESS 51

- Step One: Education 51
- Step Two: Planning 54
- Step Three: Buy The Right Property 54
- Step Four: Team Building 56
- Step Five: Circle of Influence 60
- Step Six: The Right Sellers 61
- Step Seven: Hobby/Business? 61
- Step Eight: Stick With It 62

COMMON PITFALLS AND HOW TO AVOID THEM 63

CONCLUSION 74

Introduction

Real estate investing is one of the popular forms of investment that can help you generate income and secure both your current and future life. For some, it is considered one of the simplest and easiest forms of investment as it is perceived as an exchange of property between two owners. The property is afterward rented out and the rent keeps on coming securing a stable income every month. The truth, however, is that property investment is much more complicated than that. If you are a beginner, I strongly recommend that you get familiar with the process prior to putting your money in the property market. You need to understand the basic factors of investment, what are the possible risks and the overall economic situation at the moment.

Through real estate investing, many individuals just like you have been able to increase their net worth substantially, obtain the things they always wanted to have, reached their financial goals faster than they thought possible, and preserved their wealth for their retirement and/or their families. And many have done so without much money to start with, or without any money to start with at all. The fact is, real estate investing is a powerful tool for building and preserving wealth no matter where you live and no matter who you are. And unlike some investment opportunities, real estate investing has "staying power."

Demand for real estate in most areas is constant although there are economic factors that influence the market and its demands. The good news is that when the economy is in a slump, there are tremendous opportunities for good real estate deals because the number of buyers decreases along with tougher economic times. Now is just such a time and that makes investing in real estate more lucrative than ever. The key to building wealth through real estate is having the knowledge to understand the market swings and pressures and then being able to capitalize on the opportunities as you find them. There will always be an never-ending supply of buyers looking for everything from their first home to their retirement home - and you will be the investor who has exactly what these buyers need.

Basically, in order to be a successful real estate investor, the profit that you make should be higher than the taxes you pay and the overall maintenance cost of owning the property. You need to know what are the different types of properties that you can invest in, how you can make money from your investment and what are the common pitfalls that you need to avoid. The guide that I have compiled below will help you understand the basics of real estate investing and make it easier, to begin with, this undertaking.

About The Book

In writing "How to Invest in Real Estate", my intent has been to cover all topics that first-time real estate investors need to know - but to do so in less depth than I've included in my title.

Here you'll find discussions about types of real estate investments, ways of investing in real estate, steps to investment success and few other topics. In this book, you'll gain a profit-generating introduction to the complete range of knowledge you'll need to begin building wealth in the real estate.

In other words, the another title for this book might have been Real Estate Investing in a Nutshell. This book is directed toward those readers who want to sample all investment topics in one easy-to-read volume.

Either way, whether you select this abridged volume or some combination of my other titles, you'll find that I offer my readers the most detailed and practical guide to investing in real estate that is available. Although I am quite optimistic on your opportunities to build wealth with property, I never mislead my readers into believing that this wealth will come without knowledge, time, and effort. It's certainly true.

You can get rich in the real estate but you must learn how to analyze properties, neighborhoods, and financial risks and rewards. And that's exactly what my books will help you learn.

What Is Real Estate?

Real estate is property consisting of land, the buildings on it, and any natural resources within the property boundaries, such as minerals waters and crops. Real estate can be categorized into four types: residential, commercial, industrial, and land.

Residential properties include structures for domestic residence such as single-family homes, condominiums, townhouses, mobile homes, and vacation rentals. Commercial properties include structures used to produce income such as offices, stores, hotels, services, and other businesses. Industrial properties include structures used manufacturing, such as factories, warehouses, and research centers. Generally industrial is for the production of goods and commercial is for the distribution of goods. Land properties include few or no structures such as vacant land, farms, ranches, and reclaimed sites.

The Academic Definition

Real estate has been defined as land or immovable property along with anything permanently affixed to the land such as buildings and investment is the act of using money to purchase property for the sole purpose of holding or leasing for income. It is safe to say then that real estate investing involves the acquisition of real estate (or investment in real estate) for purposes of generating income, making a profit, and acquiring wealth.

The Conceptual Definition

- Leverage - In contrast to stock investments which usually require more equity from the investor, it is possible to leverage a real estate investment. With a real estate investment, you can use other people's money to magnify your rate of return and control a much larger investment otherwise, not possible.
- Tax Shelter - Real estate investing provides tax benefits. There are yields on annual after-tax cash flows, equity buildup through appreciation of the asset, and cash flow after tax upon sale.
- Non-Monetary Returns - Real estate investment provides pride of ownership, the security that you control ownership, and portfolio diversification.

It's a competitive world out there. There are many investment options. So why should you invest in real estate? Well, the real estate has some unique qualities that have made it one of the top investment strategies for hundreds of years. Its benefits include:

You can get paid two times - instead of once like most other investments. In real estate, you get money from both the operation of the property (also known as a "dividend") and a second time when you sell it, and its value has increased due to increasing rents (known as "capital appreciation"). This is in contrast to most other investments such as precious metals and non-dividend paying stocks, in which you only get paid once based on appreciation of the value of the asset. For example, if you buy an ounce of gold, you don't get a penny in dividends. The only thing you get is the difference between what you bought the gold for and what you sell it for. The same is true for most stocks. Clearly, the best of all worlds is to get consistent income while you own it, and then a large distribution when you sell it.

It pays a higher dividend than any other form of investment. Most real estate investments pay out a dividend of roughly 10%. The average stock that pays a dividend - and most don't - is lucky to be 1%. The same is true with CDs and bonds - you are looking at around 3% to 5%. There are no other forms of investing that can pay out a dividend as high as real estate. Of course, there are such items as "junk bonds" that might pay out 10%, but they might just as likely lose your entire investment if they default. That's why they call them "junk". Remember the saying "before you can have return on investment, there must be return of investment".

It comes with attractive leverage. Most real estate investments include the potential for leverage in the form of a mortgage. This allows the investor to create an even higher return, without taking excessive risk. If you buy a property and put down 20%, and borrow the remaining 80%, you will increase the yield on your investment hugely, assuming that the yield of the entire property is higher than the interest rate of the mortgage. This ability to utilize intelligent leverage has long been an attraction. It allows you to pay off the property using the property's own cash flow. Can you do this with a CD? No. Bond? No. Gold? No. Sure, you can buy stock on margin, but that is really a form of speculation more than investing, and often has dire consequences.

It is time-proven and has an impressive track record. Investing in real estate has an impressive pedigree. The first American millionaire - John Jacob Astor - made his fortune in Manhattan real estate. Since then, many of the richest individuals in the U.S. have created their wealth in real estate. These include Donald Trump, Conrad Hilton, Joseph Kennedy, and literally hundreds of thousands more. It has been asserted that more wealth has been created through real estate investing than all other forms of investing combined.

Security. When you invest in a stock or bond, you don't have any control over where your money goes or how that company is managed. Unlike Warren Buffet, who normally buys full control of the entity through buying a majority of the stock, the regular investor has no power over the day-to-day operations of the business they own stock or bonds in. Additionally, their stock or bonds are normally not secured by anything tangible. In most cases, all you have as security on your investment is a piece of paper and the hope that there will be a market of buyers for that piece of paper in the future. With the real estate, you get a deed to a property - the title to the asset is put in your name. You control what happens. You are the boss. Your investment - your capital - is backed by the title to real estate.

You can use your super. Self-managed super funds have been around for some time – however, it's only in recent years that investing in property via super has emerged as a feasible option due to changes in the law regarding borrowing. It's incredibly tax-effective: CGT on sale is just 10%, and zero if you're over 60; a recent ATO ruling also means you're now allowed to renovate properties held within the fund too. However, you do have to stay within the rules, which are quite complex, so seek advice before going down this route.

It's easier to hold onto if things go wrong. Margin calls are a common feature of shareholdings: essentially, if you've borrowed to invest in share, the margin call is when you are asked to deposit more money if the assets in your portfolio fall below a certain amount. However, it's almost unheard of for a lender to ask you to top up a mortgage if a property falls in value – as long as you can keep up the repayments, you'll be able to continue holding your property until its value increases again.

It's an asset you can use. Investment or not, your property is still just that – a property. So should events take a turn which means you have to move into that property, you can (pending rental agreements, of course) whether for the short term or the long term - and, if things change again, you can move back out, leaving your investment intact. That's a hard thing to do with a share certificate or a bar of gold.

Not just investors in the market. An important factor in the robustness of the property market is the fact that it's not just investors buying and selling property - in fact, investors are the minority. Investors account for around 30% of all mortgages taken out, with the remaining 70% by homeowners – who aren't necessarily buying with the principal aim of making money from property, but due to any number of reason. This provides the housing market with a base 'floor' of activity which, while not protecting it from ups and downs, does limit their impact somewhat.

As long as people choose to live in houses, units & apartments, residential property will always be stable. From the young couple who have saved enough for a deposit, to the investor renting student accommodation through to the downsizer and retirement village, residential property is always sought after.

Demand is outstripping supply. Linked to this is that there is an ongoing demand for property - both rental property and property to buy. Population is growing and housing supply remains tight in many areas (particularly capital cities and areas affected by the resources boom). This provides another floor under the market which makes it less likely that prices will crash. Do your research carefully, though, as some areas of the market do experience oversupply.

Limited immunity from fluctuation. Another experienced investor and market commentator, Margaret Lomas, argues that the right kind of property can also offer limited immunity against recession. During an economic slowdown, more demand from both buyers and tenants falls into lower markets. This increases values and yields.

Other people pay for your investment. In fact, it's worth noting that, as well as being able to borrow the vast majority of the asset value and the tax benefits, you're also getting other people – namely tenants - to subsidize your investment through rental payments. You're getting three different parties helping you make money through capital gain (or cash flow) – making property one of the most affordable investments around.

Still keep growing even when you're retired. Many investors following a capital growth strategy are putting together a nest egg for their retirement - whether that's based on selling down and creating a lump sum, partially selling down and living off rental income, or on living off a line of credit. However, what some investors forget is that, even after they retire in, say, 20 years, yield and value will continue to improve – making you worth more each year.

It's a more stable investment. The property market is usually much less volatile than the share market, at least partly due to the effort required in order to purchase a property – in terms of due diligence, legal checks, inspections, length of settlement periods and so on. This means that property is less prone to short-term speculators than paper asset classes. This along with the relatively long amount of time it takes to liquidate a property asset – also reduces market volatility significantly. Properties in well-located areas, underpinned by good supply and demand, rarely crash overnight or even over extended periods of time. They hold their own or at least level off and rarely experience major falls. Investors can avoid high-risk areas simply by researching suburbs and properties well before they buy.

You benefit from other people's spending. Specifically, government and company investment. Spending on infrastructures like roads and rail and airports can boost values in a suburb or regional town which may have previously had accessibility issues; meanwhile, investment in new premises or projects – universities, hospital factories, resources projects, shopping centers and so on - can provide employment opportunities and increase housing demand. New amenities can also see house prices increase, purely down to an area becoming a nicer place to live. And that all happens without you having to spend a cent.

Investors provide housing. Financial benefits not enough for you? Well, how about social benefits? Investing in property provides a supply of rental housing at a range of budget levels - meaning those that either can't or choose not to buy a property have a choice of places in which to live. Without property investors, providing rental housing would be solely down to the government - you're housing the nation.

You can pass it onto your kids. When thinking long-term for your investment, you don't just have to think your lifetime – you can also think about your children too. Depending on the legal structure in which you own your properties, you can pass your investments onto your children either before or after you pass away. Sure, you can do this with shareholdings too, but how many top companies from 30 years ago are still at the top of the ASX 200? Not that many - whereas a well-positioned property should continue to grow over the long term.

You don't have to do the dirty work. If the idea of property hunting, renovating, developing, dealing with tenants or any of the associated tasks that come along with investing in property don't appeal to you, then you don't need to do them. The property industry is well-established, with the ability to outsource pretty much every task to an eager – and competent – service provider such as buyers agents, builders, property managers, and so on. Sure, it may cost you – but the best providers also confer a competitive advantage which can actually boost your profits.

Is Real Estate A Good Investment?

Owning a home is the American Dream, but is buying additional real estate a good investment? It can be so long as you have realistic expectations.

There are a lot of investment strategies out there, so why would real estate be on the table? The reason most people invest in real estate is the long term gain. Only in rare cases, such as flipping a home, will you make a killing in a year. In most cases, you make the big return over a longer period of time by paying down the mortgage and watching the home appreciate. Investing in rentals is popular because the renters tend to pay off your mortgage for you.

Real estate investment tends to be much more robust and stable and can grow your wealth. While the demand and market fluctuations, people will always need a place to live and therefore demand even in tough economic times will exist. It is ideal to invest in real estate when the economy is weak as more people cannot afford to purchase their own homes. Hence, they try to save their credit or avoid foreclosure by unloading their homes at prices much below market value.

It is a known fact that most properties will increase in selling price or value depending on its location as long as you are willing to do the work in renting it out while you wait for a seller's market. As your property's value increases over time, your possible earnings increase too depending on several factors like where your property is situated, what kind of property is it, upkeep and many other factors. Investing in stable real estate, however, will increase the likelihood of your property to have a higher value in the future. Doing this right definitely requires training from someone with experience.

Opting for real estate as an investment can give you great returns and benefits. Rental properties create a steady source of income that you can quickly appreciate in value with minor changes. You may need to put out some money in purchasing the property and fixing it but you can quickly see a return on investment since you will be earning money and equity monthly from your rental property. Take into account that benefit of leverage that pertains to your capacity to purchase a rental property using your own cash or loans from a financial institution by using the equity from your other properties. However, use caution when using this technique as if you overdo it, you can own dozens of properties and still end up up-side-down on your mortgages.

Leverage enables you to invest in additional rental properties and save for maintenance and upkeep of your existing properties. The advantage is that you only pay for a part of the mortgage or none if you've learned how to get good renters. Now, not only will your property increases your profits every month as rental return pays down the mortgage, but you'll also be gaining equity. Yet another benefit provided by a rental property is deductions in tax, which will enable you to take away or reduce the cost of repairs and maintenance, insurance, improvements, mortgage interest and much more.

You are even your own boss and it is your own business. A lot of people find this kind of investment very rewarding and that is why it is always on top no matter how weak the economy is, but remember if you do this wrong and just 'wing it' you can get 'hosed.' I've prepared some powerful investment information for you below, enjoy.

Type Of Real Estate Investing

Real estate investments done right can be lucrative and rewarding. For someone who is thinking about getting involved and building a portfolio, it's important to know about the different types of investment, including the pros and cons of each. Having a good understanding of the different types of real estate investment can help you decide what real estate investment right for you.

Residential Real Estate

Residential real estate is the type of real estate that involves single family and multi-family properties, including duplexes and triplexes. The most common type of residential real estate is single-family homes. Single-family properties tend to have the greatest number of buyers and are the easiest to market to the general population.

People who invest in single family homes may rent out the property. As long as the home is occupied, it will generate income. However, if the tenant moves away, a single-family home will generate no income until another tenant moves in. For this reason, many residential investors that don't want to make their investments a full-time job opt to have a property management company help retain and funnel in tenants.

A multi-family property is different because it will generate income as long as some of the units are occupied. These buildings are more difficult to sell and can take longer to find a buyer, but they represent a more sure way to make an income on an investment property when occupied.

Real estate investors hoping to maximize their profits on their multi-family building can live in their building and enjoy an owner-occupied mortgage at a special rate.

Fix and Flip Properties

Some real estate investors choose to purchase residential real estate, fix it for a low cost, and sell the house at a profit. Fix and flip properties are typically sold at a discounted price because they're in poor shape and can be sold at a much higher rate after they're fixed. Fix and flip properties work well for home buyers who have some knowledge of how to repair residential properties, but they hold quite a bit of risk. Looking for a home to flip is much harder than it looks on TV, and it should not be a decision made on a whim.

Commercial Real Estate

Commercial real estate like office buildings are often rented with multi-year leases that lock in revenue streams and provide stability for the property owner. Typically, a property owner will divide an office building into multiple units and rent to many different businesses. Small and medium-sized businesses are common clients in commercial real estate.

Commercial real estate is believed to have a higher and more stable income potential than residential real estate properties. Since leases are multi-year, and one building can be divided into many different units, the occupancy rate is often more stable than single family residences.

People thinking about investing in commercial real estate must do their due diligence to ensure that their investment is sound. Market research about local businesses and the property location can help investors decide whether or not an investment is a good one.

Retail Space

Retail space consists of single-use and multi-use buildings for restaurants, big box stores, strip malls, and shopping malls. Profitability from retail space is directly related to the economy and the success of the store. In some cases, leases even allow the landlord to collect a percentage based on profits from the store.

Like office space, the most stable income to be had from retail space is multi-use properties, because even if one store moves away or goes out of business, other stores will continue to generate revenue. Even more so than office buildings, location is critical for retail space, as customers must be enticed to travel there to do business.

Industrial Real Estate

Industrial real estate consists of warehouses and factories, storage businesses and distribution centers. Industrial real estate can be very lucrative for the property owner who accommodates the special needs of the client. Many tenants, in Mountain's Edge or elsewhere, are willing to pay high fees for special on-site services and features. In recent years, industrial real estate has been in high demand due to the success of online shopping and the move away from retail.

Land

Land is what lays under all those skyscrapers you see in overcrowded cities and under all suburban houses. All types of real estate investments began with land. Knowing that land appreciates just as rapidly as the properties that are located on it drives more and more real estate investors into this investment strategy. The key determinants to lands' value are location and future use. Knowing the zoning laws and criteria in your county can help guide you in making a lucrative purchase. It's good to keep in mind that cities are constantly expanding and what is an empty land now may be full of houses and buildings in less than a decade.

Mobile Homes

Mobile homes - this type of investment is perhaps more popular in the USA. If you invest in owning a mobile homes park you own the land and/or the mobile homes. Thus, you receive rent for both the land and the homes.

It is a good idea to include different types of property in your portfolio. If you are a beginner, it is better to start with residential properties as the investment in the other types is more complicated and you will benefit from having a bit of experience in the field prior to trying it out.

Earning More On The Side

If you're here, maybe you're already an agent and feeling the pinch. Maybe the first year didn't go as planned. A few deals fell through and you're feeling glum.

Real estate is a roller coaster of good times and bad times. They all seem to come in waves. Hopefully, you've planned well and set realistic income goals for your real estate. But you need to decide early if it is time for a side job, or maybe a full job. Perhaps a full job from which you can still do real estate and begin building your business there.

Few of these side jobs are guaranteed income. If you can't make another six months in the business, I recommend exploring a full-time job that can keep the lights on and the mortgage paid up. But if you still have a short runway, or are a real estate professional looking to diversify your income and restless with the usual grind, read on for ideas to make more money than just real estate commissions.

Real Estate Virtual Assistant

Put your real estate skills, training, and perhaps even license to use as a real estate virtual assistant. There are numerous companies to choose from that are growing quickly. Some companies focus on employees but others hire exclusively US-based VAs (especially for roles involving the telephone).

Real Estate Photography/Videography

If you have a talent and taste for photography, video, or drones, there is money to be made doing that part time or full time for other agents. There are numerous growing real estate photography companies who are looking for photographers to hire in-house with all the support. Or you can advertise yourself on a site like Stilio. Or you can just browse your local MLS or Zillow for listings with lousy photos. Those are the agents worth reaching out to

Real Estate Entrepreneurship

Are you a natural at staging? Do you prefer computer stuff and handling real estate transactions? Maybe you're great at real estate photography. You're an agent and a reliable handyman capable of doing contractor work?

All of these can be spun off into businesses of their own, serving other agents and businesses in your community.

Coaching and Training

If you are really good at real estate or a particular aspect of real estate, you can make money teaching it! That's what the agents who founded the Paperless Agent did – a real estate consultant program all about becoming a tech-savvy agent.

Some agents have monetized their networking and online community building skills, like the folks at Lab Coat Agents, who manage one of real estate's largest and most active Facebook groups.

Joining the Major Players

If you've met with some success in real estate, and perhaps had some coaching yourself, diversifying your income and time with some coaching is a popular way to go. You can join one of the major outfits around the country that will link you up with clients.

Course Instructor

Relatedly, you might look at classroom real estate license instruction, or teaching accreditations, designations, and continuing education courses with State and local associations. Different states have different requirements on becoming an instructor. I recommend starting by reaching out to your local association.

Writing for Real Estate

I believe content marketing has a bright future in real estate that will outlive even the traditional sales agent. Writing is a big part of content marketing and can mean a few different things.

Top teams and brokerages pay a premium for website content that is customized to them and their conversion needs. Often these companies may hire in house, or perhaps from a content company that hires the writers for them.

I recommend browsing LinkedIn jobs for the keywords "real estate writer". There are numerous types of organizations that need blog, email, or professional content. One of the best ways into a job like this is probably doing a few free guest posts. If you have what it takes, you can then perhaps parlay that into career opportunities in the future.

Affiliate Marketing

If you are website and SEO savvy, writing content for your own niche website can be a way of making money. It can be on real estate or not. When you have enough website traffic, you can partner with different products in your niche, or even Amazon, to collect affiliate commissions when people click through your site to purchase the items. Famous examples of affiliate websites include This Is Why I'm Broke, the Wirecutter, and FitSmallBusiness.

Affiliate marketing is not the only way of making money from these sites. You can enable Google AdSense, create and sell your own products (e.g. an e-book), sell advertising or sponsored advertising, and use it to become an authority in your niche.

If you are interested in a strategy like this, I recommend getting started with Authority Hacker, a blog and podcast about creating quality, long-lived, and profitable online content.

Monetize Your Existing Channels

Whether you're strapped for cash, or just looking to boost your ROI, look at what you already are doing or have that you aren't making money from. Do you have a drone that you use once a month? What if you loaned it out to other agents in your office?

Do you have a YouTube channel with 1000+ subscribers? Why not enable YouTube ads? Relatedly, if you have an awesome website that gets 10,000s+ of monthly views, you solicit ads with local businesses or even enable Google AdWords.

If you are a real estate broker, maybe it's time to set up property management and start better monetizing those leads you had been referring out previously.

Working on a Team or Salary

So, this isn't quite a side hustle. But especially if you are newer or feel in over your head, you might want to consider joining a team as a salaried agent. Your share of the split will be tiny. But you'll have a steady stream of business with the right team, and can learn the ropes of how a great functioning team is run.

You should already know some of the top teams in your market, but you can also check out Real Tends 1000 for top producing teams across the country. Not just teams, but you might also explore brokerages that pay agents by salary, like Redfin. You're still an agent, but you won't go months without a commission check.

There are other full-time jobs closely related to real estate that might be an easy transition like working for a title company, as a local builder's representative, or mortgage officer.

NAR and MLS Jobs

If you are looking for something different, but still close to home, transitioning into a role with the trade associations or MLS companies might be a natural move. NAR posts positions at both the national level as well as lets the local associations advertise open positions on their site. And of course, the MLSs need staff as well. CRMLS, BrightMLS, MFRMLS, and your local MLSs might all be a source for a real estate job or role.

Joining the Enemy

Unless you are nuts, you've been paying close attention to real estate tech and news. There is a lot going on. Some agents consider these disruptors the "enemy", foes who are trying to take agents' jobs and commissions.

These aren't just software nerds in Silicon Valley running the show. Especially with the iBuyer craze, these companies increasingly need boots on the ground and are hiring experienced agents with real estate chops. Curious about who has been hiring? Check out the list of the fastest growing real estate technology companies.

Meanwhile, the big brokerages still need employees and help, too. EXP Realty has tons of support staff for their agents, all while working in their virtual world from home. KW, Realogy, Berkshire Hathaway all are advertising staff jobs and roles.

There are different ways to earn extra income as an agent than just chasing commissions and closings. Or you can even replace your income altogether with a new real estate career. I recommend diversifying your income, even if just as a hobby. Take on a side gig! It will keep your skills sharp, expand your resume, introduce you to more people, and better protect you against industry and technological disruption.

Variety of Ways to Invest in Real Estate

There are a wide variety of ways to make great money in the world today and one of these ways is through the world of real estate. When you are considering this area you need to realize that there are a variety of advantages that you will not be able to find within other money making avenues. One of the main ones being that when you lock on to a property it becomes your very own investment and you will have total control of that asset. This gives you the ability to repair, modify, and improve your asset in any way that you see that you can make a huge profit on your total investment.

One of the most important principles that you need to know when you are looking into investing in real estate is that you need to be sure that you are buying low and selling high. Your primary objective is to locate those properties that you will be able to purchase well under market value. There are a variety of different ways that you can do this so that you are making the best deals.

With that being said, there are eight primary strategies for generating a real income in real estate. Whether you can earn a passive income or active income depends on the strategy that you implement.

Long-Term Residential Rentals

A long-term or buy-and-hold real estate strategy is a strategy used by real estate investors to purchase properties, rent them out and hold them for the long haul, typically five or more years. The long-term real estate strategy is the most common type of real estate strategy because it's generally considered easier than fixing and flipping properties because no experience is necessary, and you can hire professionals to help manage your properties.

A long-term real estate strategy can be a good way for beginners to get involved in real estate investing. It's also a solid strategy for experienced investors who want to build wealth over time from property appreciation and equity buildup.

There are several types of long-term investing. These include things like investing in turnkey real estate and apartment buildings.

Types of long-term real estate investing strategies include investing in:

- **Turnkey real estate:** Purchase a move in ready property outside of your neighborhood that usually

comes with tenants and a property management company in place.
- **Vacation rental property:** Invest in a vacation property that offsets some of the costs of home ownership by bringing in rental income.
- **Multifamily property:** Purchase a property with 2-4+ units and rent it out for rental income.
- **Apartment building:** Purchase a property that typically has 5+ units and creates monthly rental income and other income like vending and parking revenue.
- **Commercial real estate:** Purchase a property that is used for business purposes like an office building, retail store or hotel.

There are typically five benefits that you can realize by investing in buy-and-hold properties that make them beneficial for long-term investors. Some of these benefits include passive income, tax deductions, equity buildup and more.

Here are the five benefits of investing in buy-and-hold real estate:

Monthly Income on Buy-and-Hold Real Estate. One of the main benefits of buy-and-hold real estate investing is monthly rental income and any other revenue the property generates like vending, laundry and parking income. This income is considered passive income and typically is accounted for on a monthly basis.

To make sure you're collecting as much rental income as possible, you need to set your rent price correctly. If you want to figure out how much you should charge for rent, check out our rental market analysis.

Depreciation/Deductions on Buy-and-Hold Real Estate. There can be tremendous tax advantages that come from owning buy-and-hold real estate. These include things like being able to write off certain expenses like depreciation as well as mortgage interest and loan origination fees deduction. Property tax benefits are another major advantage of buy-and-hold real estate investing.

Build Equity in the Properties You Hold. With buy-and-hold investments, your tenant is paying down your mortgage for you, meaning the equity in your property typically increases each month. Furthermore, tenants will even pay your interest expense, which is tax deductible. Therefore, it's important to find good tenants who make prompt and on-time payments.

Appreciation of Buy-and-Hold Real Estate. Even though your properties can fluctuate in value, it's a safe bet that a good property located in a good area will go up steadily in value over a long period of time. This is in contrast to short-term rehab investors who might renovate a property with the expectation that appreciation will happen more quickly. Typical appreciation of buy-and-hold real estate is between 3 percent and 5 percent yearly.

Leverage on long-term Real Estate. Because you can borrow money to buy rental properties, you are able to multiply how many properties you can buy. With only a modest down payment, you are able to purchase a valuable piece of real estate. Further, you can leverage existing equity to take advantage of home equity loans and lines of credit.

While flipping a house can generate a profit, it doesn't create any passive income, doesn't have any tax advantages, doesn't build long-term equity, and leverage doesn't have much of a long-term effect. For the person looking for long-term wealth creation, buy-and-hold wins hands-down.

Lease Options

Mention "real estate investing strategies" and the first thing that typically comes to mind is buying and selling. But a strategy often overlooked and underutilized is the option - and the smart use of options can generate some fast and impressive profits.

An option gives the buyer the right but not the obligation to buy - but the seller is obligated to sell. Combine the option with a lease, and you have an excellent tool to use when you have a motivated seller with little or no equity in the property, or one who doesn't have time to wait for the traditional sales process to run its course. Instead of buying, you lease the property with an option to buy. That gives you control of the property and lets it generate cash for you - but you don't have to own it.

The rate of residential foreclosures in on the rise in many parts of the country. A pending foreclosure for any reason is just one of many situations where lease option strategies can be used. Other situations include sellers seeking debt relief or facing personal situations such as a divorce.

Why do people use lease options instead of an outright sale? Owner/sellers are likely to consider a lease option when they need to get rid of the property but do not have enough equity to sell immediately through traditional methods. For example, if the property has mortgages of up to 95 and even 100 percent of its market value, the seller would have to come up with cash to pay a real estate agent's commission. On the other side, buyers who have flawed credit, who may need time to come up with a down payment, or who want to "test drive" the house or the neighborhood are all candidates for a lease/option deal.

One of the most common option strategies is the sandwich lease option, which works like this: You lease a property with an option to buy in three years. You find a tenant/buyer who leases the property from you with an option to buy in two years. When the tenant/buyer is ready to close, you exercise your option, buy the property and sell it to the tenant/buyer.

There are, of course, possible variations. You can use different time frames. You can assign your option to the tenant/buyer or to another investor. You can buy the property instead of leasing it, and then sell it with a lease option arrangement instead of putting a traditional tenant in the house.

Focus your lease option efforts on desirable neighborhoods - generally, working-, middle-, and upper-income areas. These are the areas where potential tenant/buyers want to own homes. Also, remember that lease options can work on multi-unit buildings as well as single-family homes. If someone wants to get rid of a small apartment building and is having trouble finding a buyer, he may be willing to lease option it to you. You get into the property for a smaller-than-normal down payment and you benefit from the cash flow while you're working on the financing over a year or two or more.

Laws regarding real estate options vary by state and it's a good idea to check with a real estate attorney in your state to be sure are in full compliance with all applicable regulations when you put together a lease option transaction.

It is important to be aware that there are some risks involved with this strategy (as with all real estate investments), but there are also ways to minimize your exposure and the rewards that can come with this technique truly outweighs the risks. Real Estate investing is truly the quickest and best way to build lasting wealth. Many of the world's wealthiest people acquire much of their wealth through investing in real estate.

While lease options can build you tremendous wealth, they usually shouldnot be considered a short-term investing strategy. I define a short-term strategy as the time that passes from the start of the transaction to completion (cashing out) being less than one year.

A classic example of this would be a "rehabbing project" (fixing up a home and reselling it). The other side of the spectrum would be a longer-term strategy, such as buying a rental property and renting it over many years. I consider lease options and subject to's to be in the center of that spectrum, usually requiring one to three years for the best payoff.

However, you can always immediately sell the deal to another individual or investor for a profit; this is what is called in the business "wholesaling." This can be done if you buy the property at a low enough price that you can turn a profit by selling the deal to another investor at a discounted price.

Home-Renovation Flips

House flipping is when a real estate investor buys houses and then sells them for a profit. In order for a house to be considered a flip, it must be bought with the intention of quickly reselling. The time between the purchase and the sale often ranges from a couple months up to a year.

There are two different types of house flipping:

- An investor buys a property that has potential to increase in value with the right repairs and updates. After completing the work, they make money from selling the home for a much higher price than what they purchased it for.
- An investor buys a property in a market with rapidly rising home values. They make no updates, and after holding the property for a few months, they resell at a higher price and make a profit.

Flipping a house may sound simple, but it's not as easy as it looks. Let's be real: A house flip can either be a dream or a disaster. Done the right way, a house flip can be a great investment. In a short amount of time, you can make smart renovations and sell the house for much more than you paid for it. But a house flip can just as easily go the wrong direction if it's done the wrong way. We've all heard house flipping horror stories - the ones where what seemed like a good deal turned into a house with a shaky foundation and a leaking roof. At the end of the day, a house flip may not make you money. It actually could cost you thousands. If you decide to flip a house, you certainly don't want to lose money. You want to make a wise investment and reap the rewards.

Steps to Flipping Houses

Step 1: Do The Research

Before you jump into your New Year's Resolution of making more money, there is some work you need to do. The first rule in House Flipping 101 is read everything you can get your hands on. Educate yourself about flipping houses and listen to podcasts. You could even take an experienced flipper out to lunch and pick their brain.

Step 2: Find The Right Location

Part of your research should involve finding the right neighborhood for your investment. Find out where people want to live and what kind of houses buyers are looking for in this area. Don't settle for a sketchy area just because the house seems like it's a good deal. Buying a home in a less than desirable area will cost you more in the long run. The longer it sits empty because buyers don't like the neighborhood, the more you're paying in monthly fees to maintain it. Be familiar with real estate market trends in your area. Don't assume that the upgrades and marketing strategies that worked for real estate in your hometown of New Jersey will work the same for the South Tampa homes or the Miami investment property that you're thinking about flipping. Each city, state, and neighborhood has a particular audience, and if you don't give them what they're looking for, you'll waste a lot of time and money.

Step 3: Get Your Finances In Order

Once you know what you want to do, you have to get all of your financial ducks in a row. This means improving your credit score if it's low and acquiring the cash required for a down payment. This way, once you find the perfect house, you can make an offer right away. Be realistic about how much house you can afford. The less money you put into buying the home, the more you have to spend on upgrades.

Step 4: Remodeling

In order to attract buyers, chances are pretty fair that you'll need to remodel the house before you can flip it. Remodeling the house is a process which should be done with a strict budget in mind and is crucial to your success as a real estate investor.

Just like when buying the property, controlling your costs in the rehab phase is just as important in order to maintain as much of your profits as you possibly can. Whether you use a general contractor on your team or if you use subs and you are the general contractor, you are the one to control the budget set forth between you and your rehab team.

Using a budget repair form is a good way to keep track of the repairs needed as a snapshot is a very effective way to control costs. And you should use this form when getting estimates from multiple subcontractors like electricians, plumbers, framers, finish carpenters and painters. Once you've received all estimates from the subcontractors and finalized the pricing, then lay out a timeline for completion. At this stage, you must do everything in your power to hold all the subcontractors accountable for the prices they gave you so you don't go over the budget.

Step 5: Sell and Profit

The final step on how to flip a house successfully is the most obvious one...sell! This is the part where all your hard work pays off if you did everything else correctly. And although there are many house flippers who like to do this themselves, I don't recommend it. Unless you are a real estate broker or if you are fully equipped to put some serious effort in doing this yourself, the best way to flip a house successfully in this final stage is to hire a real estate agent to list and sell the house.

To find a qualified real estate agent, look to your contacts. Chances are you probably already have some relationships built up when you were first looking to buy. Use those same real estate resources. No matter what you do however, make sure that the real estate agent has a solid marketing plan to sell your property as quick as possible. This may include:

- MLS
- Signs
- Direct Mail
- Open Houses
- Newspaper Ads
- Internet Marketing and Facebook

Interview as many real estate agents as you can until you are comfortable that the plan they have is one that will sell the house quickly. In the meantime, you can be on the lookout for your next house to flip while your real estate broker is marketing this one.

Contract Flipping

One way that you can make money from real estate without having to put up very much capital or credit is to flip contracts. All you have to do is find a distressed seller and a motivated buyer and bring them all together. While locating a distressed seller might seem difficult, Clothier has systemized the entire process for doing this. The trick with contract flipping is to identify the distressed seller and locate a ready-to-go buyer.

By bringing these parties together, you've cut out the need to go hunting for a buyer after you've entered a contract. That situation presents more risk. Instead, by locating the sellers and the buyers beforehand, you can easily enter into a contract with the confidence that you won't get stuck having to close escrow on the property.

To do this, you have to be able to identify either vacant homes or homes that are behind on their mortgages. That's the tricky part. You're effectively trying to find distressed sellers. But homes that are already vacant are primed for an opportunity like this.

Short Sales

A short sale is the sale of a real estate property for which the lender is willing to accept less than the amount still owed on the mortgage.

For a sale to be considered a short sale, these two things must be true:

- The homeowner must be so far behind on payments that they can't catch up.
- The housing market must have gone down so much that the house is worth less than the remaining balance on the mortgage.

In most cases, the lender (and the homeowner) will try a short sale process in order to avoid foreclosure. Overall, there are a lot of misunderstandings around short sales. But one common misconception is that lenders just want to be rid of the property and will move quickly to get as much money back as possible.

In reality, the lender will take their time to recover as much of their loss as they can. Here's the thing: Just because a property is listed as a short sale does not mean the lender has to accept your offer, even if the seller accepts it. This is what makes the short sale process so tricky.

If you're wondering what the standard steps are that typically happen as part of the short sale process, look no further.

Step 1: The homeowner starts by talking to their lender and a real estate agent about the likelihood of selling their house via short sale. At this point, they may submit a short sale package to their lender. They'll also have to prove to their lender that they're no longer capable of making their mortgage payments and have no assets that would allow them to catch up on payments.

Step 2: The homeowner works with a real estate agent to list the property. They'll execute a sales contract for the purchase of the property once a buyer is interested. However, this contract is subject to the lender's approval and is not final until then—even if both the seller and the buyer agree on the terms.

Step 3: The lender reviews the contract and could then respond in a variety of ways. They could choose not to respond at all, they could reject the offer, they could reject the offer but outline which terms they would agree to, or they just might approve the offer.

Step 4: When the lender's response is presented to the potential buyer, the contract will either stay the same or the buyer will choose to appease or reject the lender's terms. So, at this point, the ball is in the buyer's court.

Step 5: If the contract is approved, the short sale property closes and the home is transferred to the new buyer. The lender receives all proceeds from the sale of the property and releases the original homeowner from their mortgage loan - even though the full mortgage balance was not paid off by the proceeds.

Vacation Rentals

Vacation rentals present a lucrative path to profits in the real estate marketplace. Not only can you make some side hustle income from vacation rentals, but you could potentially make a significant amount of money and build up a substantial passive income stream if you're in a highly-trafficked tourist locale. Places like Los Angeles, Miami, and other tourist hot-beds are well known for having high demand for these short-term rentals.

The best part? You don't even need to own the properties to make money. Two of the world's most successful property management companies that specialize vacation rentals like Joe Poulin's, Luxury Retreats or Michael Joseph's, Invited Home, don't actually own the homes. But they do provide a high-end consumer experience.

How do you participate? Leverage existing relationships with owners in your area. Network with others. Build bonds. Create systems. Ensure the utmost satisfaction and go above and beyond for anyone staying at the homes you'll manage. And see how you can help to take some of the time and stress off of the present owners' existing rental businesses. Or, if you have a property, list it on a site like Airbnb, HomeAway, or FlipKey before managing vacation rentals for other owners.

Hard-Money Lending

Hard-money lenders provide short-term loans to people that normally wouldn't qualify for those loans. Now, in order to participate in hard-money lending, you'll need some capital behind you. These are loans that are often at high-interest rates because they're for very brief periods. To get your first deal done, you could turn to a hard money lender. If you have a "sure thing," and you lack the capital, this is your best bet.

However, you could also become a hard money lender. Now, that means you'll need some capital. And this likely isn't going to be the first way you start making money in real estate. But as you build your network, your capital and a solid portfolio of deals, you could provide these bridge loans and make a great rate of return.

Even if you lack an enormous amount of capital, as long as you can successfully identify the right deals, provide a small amount of money and generate a high success rate, you can easily find investors to come on board. The interest rates here make sense. There's more risk, but also far more reward. It's a way to keep your cash fairly liquid and generate a nice profit in the short term without having to wait years and years for those returns to materialize.

Commercial Real Estate

Commercial real estate is a broad term describing real property used to generate a profit. Examples of commercial real estate include office buildings, industrial property, medical centers, hotels, malls, farmland, apartment buildings, and warehouses.

Historically, investing in commercial real estate as an alternative asset has provided millions of investors with attractive risk-adjusted returns and portfolio diversification. But, many investors still don't understand how commercial real estate works as an investment vehicle.

There are some key differences between commercial real estate investing and traditional investments such as stocks and bonds. Unlike stocks and bonds traded frequently on a secondary market, real estate is a scarce resource and holds intrinsic value as hard asset. Most often, stocks are purchased for their selling potential rather than their capacity as a source of income, hence the "buy low, sell high" heuristic of the stock market.

The investment strategy for commercial real estate is simple: there is inherent demand for real estate in a given area. Investors purchase the property and make money in two ways: first, by leasing the property and charging tenants rent in exchange for use of the property; and second by appreciation in the value of the property over time.

Historically, direct commercial real estate investment has been out of reach for the everyday investor. This is because investments in commercial real estate are typically dominated by institutional investors as projects require millions of dollars in capital and a deep reservoir of expertise for improving and operating a property.

8 Steps to Real Estate Investing Success

A lot of investors cannot accomplish their dreams because they cannot effectively introduce their investing professions or because they reach a crossroads and have no idea which way to turn.

Baffled about the next action to take, they spin their wheels, not do anything, and ultimately decide to ignore reality entirely and return to a life of mediocrity. To avoid this from occurring to you, follow this easy eight action roadmap to success.

Step One: Education

If you talk to enough investors or visit the many investment websites made available, you will have undoubtedly heard that education is essential. Seasoned investors may scoff at this notion, but the more you can educate yourself, the better chance you have at being successful. The mistake that is often made is thinking that education alone will make you a better investor. Sure, it will come in handy to know how to structure deals or to be able to engage in conversation with a fellow investor, but that is not the only reason why you would need to be educated. If you can educate yourself through other people's mistakes, it will save you time and money.

An education in real estate investing is about seeing how things were done in the past and what changes can be made to improve the future. You may not currently be thinking of how to buy an apartment building or how to structure seller financing, but you will at some point down the road. Instead of just winging it or asking around when the time comes, you can revert back to what you have learned from others. Familiarizing yourself with their mistakes will help you avoid making them yourself.

Investment club meetings, networking events and even real estate investing websites can serve as a great source of education. Every conversation you have with someone in the business may come back to you down the road. Listen to the keynote speaker at each investment meeting and make a mental note of what worked for them and what didn't. Talk to as many different types of investors and people in the business as you can. A mortgage broker may open your eyes to a restructuring plan that can save you hundreds of dollars a month. An attorney or accountant may show you a better way for accounting or an updated business system. A fellow investor may pique your curiosity for a different avenue to invest. The more you can learn about the business, the better you will know what works and what you may want to change or stay away from.

There is a lot to know in real estate, finance and investing. There are multiple terms in every facet of the business that can be confusing, even if you know finance and investing. It sounds simple enough, but instead of surfing around the internet for an hour, take that time to learn something new. Success favors those who are the most prepared and you never know when a deal will fall into your lap. If you have learned the process along the way, you will be much more open to the opportunity and be able to take advantage of it. You never want to learn as you go. If you take little steps every day, you will have a much greater grasp on the business in no time.

Education isn't always about being able to cite terms or meanings at the drop of a hat. Sometimes educating yourself is learning what works and what you may need to change. It is cheaper and easier to do this at another person's expense. Ask those investors who went into a deal without knowing exactly what they were doing if they value education. I think you will find that the answer is a resounding yes.

Learn enough to be able to compose a smart deal then make it happen. As your profession advances, continue learning as you go along. There's a lots of built up investing understanding offered, so benefit from it. Bear in mind, too, that education does not need to be a $2,000-$3,000 guru-sponsored super course. You can often discover more from a $20 book, but never ever give up learning or you will stop growing.

Step Two: Planning

What actions are you requiring to reach your objectives? Are you relaxing with a scratch pad and a pen preparation how you'll invest your property earnings or are you taking a series of intentional actions to all but ensure your success? The number of calls is you going to make today, today, or this month? The number of residential or commercial properties will you take a look at? The number of deals will you compose? Realty is a numbers game, so you need to plan your numbers and after that, you need to subsequent by examining your activity.

If you do not keep rating you will not know if you're winning or losing. All of it starts with a plan and ends in the winner's circle or the work workplace. Preparation – or cannot plan – will figure out where you'll remain in a year and how much money you'll have.

Step Three: Buy The Right Property

While location does the heavy lifting in your investment property's performance – owning the right property in that location is critical. That's why

I would only buy an investment grade property – one with occupier appeal, a level of scarcity, close to public transport and infrastructure and one that gives me the ability to add value and manufacture some further capital growth.

Approximately 20% of the population owns an investment property. Of those investors, 50% will sell within the next five years. Many first time investors don't buy an "investment grade" quality property and make mistakes when buying. So what are some of the common pitfalls to avoid when searching for the ideal investment?

Banks consider several investment property types as risky. These often include serviced apartments, student accommodation, defense housing, small apartments, commercial properties and properties in a business or mixed zoning or in country or outer coastal areas. Major banks occasionally don't want to lend against certain properties or restrict loan to value ratios (LVR's). Purchase these types of properties with caution. If it's not good enough for the bank's money, it shouldn't be good enough for yours.

In addition, you should watch out for properties that come with rental guarantees for a year or two. The only guarantee is that the developer has loaded the rental amount into the inflated purchase price.

Properties in certain postcodes or suburbs also have finance restrictions. Southbank, Queens Road and St Kilda Road, Docklands, Port Melbourne, South Melbourne, and Carlton are generally seen as riskier properties for the banks and will have finance restrictions.

Importantly, your property will need to be suitable for the target market of the area which you would have identified in your research.

Step Four: Team Building

Building a real estate team is no simple task, nor should it ever be taken lightly. If for nothing else, a properly assembled team can take your business to a higher level than you ever imagined. With the right people in place, there is no reason you can't expect to realize success on a higher level. And therein lies the secret to optimizing your own investing business: building a real estate team.

The smartest investors out there are well aware that they can't do everything by themselves. And while there is a lot to be said for the successful individual that runs their own business, without the help of anyone else, no one person can take the place of an entire team firing on all cylinders. If for nothing else, building a real estate team, at least one that is put together carefully, is one of the best decisions an investor can make. With the right people in place, it's entirely possible for success to become habitual and your workload to be lightened. What more could you ask for? If that doesn't sell you on building a real estate team, I don't know what will.

Everyone from your real estate agent to your repairman plays a part in your success. Consequently, neglecting to build a team with the proper components is a sure-fire strategy to put yourself "behind the eight-ball."

Instead of waiting until there is a specific need, you should take any downtime to look for the best fits for your business. It will take some time to get everyone in place, but once you do, your team will be a force in your area. If you are considering building a real estate team, may I recommend the following?

Real Estate Agent: A good real estate agent is usually behind every successful investor. They can be a great source for leads, and make you aware of deals you didn't even know existed. However, not every successful real estate agent is a fit to work with investors. You need to do your homework and find out if they are a good fit for you. Don't be afraid to ask them how and where they find new listings. Ask them if they own any investment properties themselves and if they work with other investors. Treat this as a job interview. There are plenty of real estate agents in every market. It is important that you can find one that knows your goals and can help you achieve them. Hopefully, you will work together on plenty of deals, so you also need to be comfortable with them. A good agent is an important piece in building a successful real estate team.

Contractor: If you focus on rehabs, you need a quality contractor. In much the same way that you find your real estate agent, you should look for your contractor. Odds are that you won't use the first one you talk to. You can find a contractor through personal referrals, networking meetings or local real estate clubs. Once you make contact, you should ask for references and availability. A good contractor should be able to quickly supply you with both. It is not realistic for them to drop everything they are doing for you, but you do need to feel important. Furthermore, you want to feel like you are on the same page and can work together moving forward. A good contractor can help keep you under budget and finish your projects within your time-frame.

Property Manager: If you are looking to grow your rental portfolio, you need a good property manager to run your properties. A good property manager handles projects for you and allows you to focus on other areas of your business. Finding new tenants, rent collection and scheduling regular maintenance is not only a burden but can consume most of your day. By not having to deal with these issues, your rental business can almost run itself.

Again, a good property manager is well worth what you are paying them.

Wholesalers: Real estate is very much a numbers game. You want as many different lead sources as possible. Even if you have a great real estate agent, there is always room for a quality wholesaler. Wholesalers need cash buyers that can quickly close on deals. If you can demonstrate that you are a reliable outlet for deals, your wholesaler will come to you with as many deals as they get.

Attorney: Real estate investors have essentially one goal: closing deals. Your attorney will help push the deals you are working on over the finish line. Additionally, they are there to protect you and keep your best interests in mind. Much like with your real estate agent, you need to know that your attorney works with you and how you want to invest. For starters, you should make sure that they focus on real estate. Next, you need to know that they will be available when you need them. With a good attorney behind you, it will give you the confidence to pursue deals.

Handyman: You never know when something will happen unexpectedly on a rental property. When it does, you need to be able to get someone to the house as quickly as possible. It is important that you develop a relationship with someone that can do multiple tasks for you. Not only is finding someone in a pinch time consuming but can end up being costly. A handyman can handle everything from changing locks to repairing appliances. Over time, they will end up saving you a lot of money.

Accountant: Another team member that will save you money is your accountant. Most people think that your accountant is only important at tax time. This is where they make their money, but they will also help you with budgeting and payments. If numbers are not your strong suit, you will lean on your accountant to handle everything from security deposits to bill payments.

Building a real estate team takes time. It requires you to put yourself out there and find the best talent available. With a strong team in place, your investing business will run smoothly and be as efficient as possible. What more could you possibly want?

Step Five: Circle of Influence

Who are you paying attention to? Your sibling whose idea of imaginative realty investing is purchasing a timeshare in Arkansas? If your circle of influence – people who offer you suggestions – have no idea and understand property investing, they'll continuously be taking objective on your hopes and dreams because they do not understand the idea or because they do not want your success to shine a spotlight on their mediocrity. Use as many innovative – and effective – real estate financiers as you can at your local REIA conferences.

Step Six: The Right Sellers

Wasting time aiming to browbeat someone into accepting your innovative deal is ineffective and demoralizing. Make certain that the sellers you're handling are extremely inspired to offer and good ideas will happen. Do not hesitate to leave the incorrect offer even if the rate is right. Know your perfect circumstance then profit from it when the chance emerges.

Step Seven: Hobby/Business?

Is realty investing going to be your path to success? While there are a lot of chances for you to have a good time, never ever forget that you're playing in a very competitive sandbox. You have something opting for you, however. Great deals of financiers do not have the education, training, and frame of mind to succeed. If you're one of them, you ought to save your money and use up stamp gathering or sign up with the rock club. If nevertheless, you're major about success and offer this business the effort it is worthy of, your future is a blank check – and you're holding the pen.

Step Eight: Stick With It

Real estate investing success will not always come overnight. That's not to say that you will not become an overnight experience, but be gotten ready for the possibility that it may take 3-5 years to attain a level of success that influences you to toss all your energy and time into improving yourself. Property investing is simple, but it's not basic. It takes work, effort, and a desire to keep plodding ahead even when your huge payday is years away – rather of simple days.

By following this eight step action plan you can set your sights on reaching all your personal and financial dreams. Realty investing is among the most financially rewarding professions worldwide, but you'll need to devote yourself to your success. How bad do you want it?

Common Pitfalls And How To Avoid Them

In real estate investment there probably isn't a mistake that hasn't been made. The majority of mistakes in real estate investment are made by investors just beginning in real estate who don't have enough experience in the field to avoid them. It's mistakes that stop real estate investors from continuing in real estate investing after their first investment.

Let's begin by talking about the most common real estate investment mistakes and give some advice about how you can avoid them. Feel free to share any comments below or any personal experiences that you feel would be beneficial.

Pitfall 1: Not Knowing What Your Objectives Are

If you don't know your destination, how can you plan to get there? You need to be specific before you start investing in real estate. Know why you are investing and the timescale of investment. Do you want to benefit from income now or in the future? Are you trying to build a property investment portfolio that will support you through your retired years? Do you plan to sell properties before you retire, perhaps to make more money to meet other financial responsibilities? Answering questions like these are crucial to creating a property investment plan to get you to where you want to be in life and successfully become a real estate investor.

Pitfall 2: Letting Your Emotions Get The Worst Of You

When you buy a home, your emotions begin to kick in. You just "know" and "feel" when it is the right property for you to live in. Investing in a property is a completely different story. If you let your emotions overrule property investment logic, then you are definitely going to lose money. Don't consider an investment property based on your emotions or from how beautiful the property looks or how cozy the rooms are. Consider your investment objectives and ask if this property will help in the achievement of your goals. Will it attract tenants? Will it give you a good return? Be very specific in what your goals are and don't rush into making a decision unless you're sure that this property will generate positive cash flow for you in the future.

Pitfall 3: Foolishness vs. Fear

Too much haste or too much hesitancy. There are two types of real estate investors out there: the foolish and the fearful. The foolish property investor acts in haste. They don't sleep on a deal or even second guess it. They believe everything the seller's agent tells them, and then rush to sign. Their hasty attitude will probably cost them money and blind them from seeing what a mistake they are making. On the other hand, some investors overly cautious. These types of real estate investors hesitate too much before closing a deal or making one. They hesitate and think and hesitate some more and with a blink of an eye comes someone else and takes from them what could have been a good property investment opportunity. The fearful type of investors doesn't know how to overcome their fear. They know the real estate investing game but don't have the courage to play it. You must be in between these two opposites to succeed in real estate.

Pitfall 4: Not Doing Your Due Diligence Properly

There are first-time investors who attend property auctions and buy a property at a bargain price. Months later that same property has come back to auction. It has failed to give the investor return, and he/she is now desperate to sell and cut the losses. The problem is that this real estate investor didn't do proper due diligence before buying the property. When you don't do your due diligence properly, you are likely to pay the wrong price or even worse, buy the wrong property. You need to know what type of property you want to invest in and where before making any decisions. You need to estimate and calculate the expected cash flow for the property and make sure that the property will produce as you expect. Do your due diligence correctly to avoid this pitfall and speak to local agents for help.

Pitfall 5: Getting The Wrong Financing

One of the exciting benefits of property investment is that you get to invest with borrowed money. Using a mortgage to fund your property investment allows you to profit from other people's money. It could massively increase your returns and yield on your capital investment. Get the financing wrong, though, and your profit could disappear. Your biggest monthly expenses are going to be the interest payments when you invest in property using a mortgage. Always use an experienced mortgage broker. They will know the real estate market like the back of their hand and help you avoid costly financing pitfalls.

Pitfall 6: Thinking You'll Save Money By Self-Managing Your Property

Only after investing does the game actually start and the hard work begins! You've got to find and examine tenants, make sure they pay their rent on time and keep up with maintenance issues. You'll need to organize tradespeople to attend to repair work and keep all your paperwork in order. You'll also have to make regular property inspections and maintain an updated inventory list. Managing an investment property can be hard work. Many investors fall into this misconception and think that they will save money by undergoing property management by themselves. But trust me, it's not a piece of cake as some might say. You need to hire a great investment property manager and let them have the daily trouble, while you concentrate on enjoying the benefits of investing in property.

Pitfall 7: Forgetting the Home Inspection

Some buyers might be willing to forgo a professional home inspection to get a deal to go through. This is always a mistake since a home inspection can reveal all the repairs you'll need to make and plan. How can real estate investors properly run the numbers if they aren't sure how much they'll need to spend on repairs? The answer: They can't.

Not only that, but it's possible you could get the seller to cover some of the repair costs during the negotiation process. However, this is only possible if you know what's wrong to begin with.

I suggest you walk through the home with the inspector to ask questions as they move from room to room. Continue asking until you're satisfied that you understand what they're saying. While a home inspector won't be able to give you estimates for repairs, they can often let you know approximately how much you'll pay. You can use this information to determine whether a property is worth investing in, or whether you should cut your losses and run.

Pitfall 8: Not Running the Numbers

This leads us to another common mistake rookie real estate investors make. Sometimes would-be investors get so excited about buying a property they forget to formally vet the deal. Not every property will make a good investment and some properties don't make sense at any price. For that reason, you have to sit down and run all the numbers to decide if a property is worth investing in.

At the bare minimum, you have to estimate mortgage payments, taxes, insurance, upfront repair costs, ongoing maintenance costs, and other expenses and compare them to the estimated market rent or sale price you'll receive for the property.

And don't forget to tally up and consider every expense you're likely to encounter. Not accounting for all expenses is the most frequent problem. Excluding vacancies and capital expenditures are the worst offenders. You will have a vacancy at some point, and not accounting for a month of lost rent every year (or every few years) can blow your entire profit. The same is true for big expenditures like a new roof, a new HVAC system, or a water heater.

Pitfall 9: Failing to Properly Screen Tenants

If you're investing in real estate to become a landlord, you'll want to have a plan in place to vet and screen tenants who apply for your rental. It can be difficult to spot potential problem tenants since bad renters won't tell you their shortcomings up front.

No one is going to approach you as a tenant and say, 'I'm not going to pay rent after the first month, and I'll throw diapers in the toilet and punch holes in the walls,' yet this happens far more often than you'd think when you don't screen your tenants.

You should run credit checks as well as criminal background checks on prospective tenants. In addition, you should watch out for "red flags" that could signal you may have a problem. Some things to watch out for include:

- **Tenants who want to move in right away:** While not always a bad thing, it can mean someone is getting evicted. It's also a sign of very poor planning on their part, and people who plan poorly for large things like a move will also tend to plan poorly for smaller things like paying rent on time.
- **Wanting to pay upfront for a year:** This is a huge red flag for a few reasons. First, it may mean they want to do nefarious things in your property and don't want you around. Second, it means they could be bad with money and may want to pay you

ahead of time while they have some, possibly from an inheritance or some other type of windfall.

While vetting tenants is a crucial component of any landlord business, it's important you don't unknowingly discriminate against tenants. To avoid lawsuits from the Federal Housing Administration (FHA), you will need to tread carefully when managing a rental property so that you don't unknowingly discriminate against tenants. There are the obvious protected classes; race, color, religion, sex, and national origin. The two that new landlords accidentally discriminate against are age, family, and disabilities. If you have questions about when you can deny an application from a potential renter, seek out an attorney in your state.

Pitfall 10: Not Having Enough Cash Reserves

I mentioned how you should always run the numbers when you invest in real estate, but it's also important to make sure you have cash on hand to pay for big expenses you anticipate (e.g., a new roof or HVAC system) - and the surprise expenses you couldn't predict if you tried (e.g., renters destroying your property).

The important lesson here is that you should always set aside money for vacancies, repairs, upgrades, and surprise expenses. While there isn't a hard and fast rule that dictates how much you should save, some landlords say setting aside 10% of the annual rent could be sufficient. You may need to save more if you have larger expenses and component replacements coming up in the near future.

Pitfall 11: Getting Advice from All the Wrong Places

When you first start in real estate investing, it can seem like everyone has an opinion. One of the biggest rookie real estate mistakes you can make is taking these random opinions to heart. As we all know, people are more than willing to give their advice, no matter how good or bad it might be. The last thing you want to do is to buy a rental property because your real estate agent says it will make the perfect rental without running the numbers and doing your own due diligence.

When it comes to taking advice from people who have never invested in real estate before, take any "words of wisdom" with a grain of salt. The same is true when you're getting advice from someone who might benefit from the sale of the property you want to buy, like your real estate agent. Always do your own research and reach out to experienced real estate investors if there are concepts you need help understanding. You can also check out online platforms for real estate investors if you need to ask questions and get advice from people who have been through it all. The real estate investing forum at Bigger Pockets is an excellent resource when you're first getting started.

As many would say, we all learn from mistakes, but it's much less costly to learn from other people's mistakes than repeat them. By avoiding these common pitfalls made in property investment, and ensuring you continue to invest without making them, you should achieve your investment and lifestyle goals easily.

Finally, if you liked the book, I would like to ask you to do me a favor and leave a review for the book on Amazon. Just go to your account on Amazon and leave an honest review.

Conclusion

When it comes to real estate investing, there are many hopeful investors who think that it is easy to make money as a real estate investor. Yes, it can be easy, but it isn't always. Real estate investing is a risky business. Real estate markets, all across the country regularly change; therefore, you aren't given any guarantees. That is why it may be a good idea to start small, by only purchasing one or two real estate properties first. This will give you the opportunity to determine if you can be successful with real estate investing and without having to go broke finding out that you can't.

Although real estate investing is considered a risky business, there are steps that you can take to improve your chances of making money with it. Perhaps, the most important thing that you can do is educate yourself about real estate investing. Be sure to focus on more than just real estate investing in general. Be sure to learn about foreclosure properties, fixer upper properties, becoming a landlord, and such. Unfortunately, too many hopeful investors mistakenly believe that real estate investing simply involves buying real estate, but it is more than that. To be a successful real estate investor, this is a fact that you must not forget.

When it comes to familiarizing yourself with the many components of real estate investing, you will see that you have a number of different options. For instance, there are several online websites that aim to provide internet users to free information on real estate investing. There are also printed resource guides or real estate investing books that can be purchased. For more detailed information with a professional spin, you can take a real estate investment training course or class, many of which are held by successful real estate investors.

As it was previously mentioned, to make a successful career out of real estate investing, you need to be able to do more than just buy and sell properties. When it comes to real estate investment properties many properties are repaired or updated and then rented out. Most commonly the landlord in charge of making all decisions is the property owner or the investor, which could be you. For you to make money in that aspect, you would need to make sure that all of your houses or apartments were filled with tenants. Do you know how you would go about doing so? Better yet, do you think that you could do so? If not, real estate investing may not be right for you.

The above-mentioned points are points that you will want to take into consideration before quitting your current job and banking on the real estate market. Yes, real estate investing is a great way to make money, but it isn't for everyone. Your first step should involve determining whether or not it is right for you.

Thank you and good luck!

www.ingramcontent.com/pod-product-compliance
Lightning Source LLC
Chambersburg PA
CBHW030017190526
45157CB00016B/3068